PROPOSALS FOR PRINTED MATTER, INC.

These proposals were sent to Printed Matter, Inc. during the Spring of 2013, proposing editions to help with their fundraising.

Some will be realised in due course, the first of which is this book.

PROPOSAL FOR PRINTED MATTER INC.

195 10th AVENUE, NEW YORK, NY 10011, U.S.A.

FOR THE PRINTED MATTER FUNDRAISING EDITION.

December 2012.

I propose to write a group of proposals for a fundraising edition at Printed Matter, New York.
I will start to write the proposals on Saturday December 1st no earlier than 12:00am. I will them write and research the proposals over a 48 hour period and finish no later than 12:00am (midnight) on Sunday 2nd December 2012.

Peter Liversidge.

PROPOSAL FOR PRINTED MATTER INC.

195 10th AVENUE, NEW YORK, NY 10011, U.S.A.

FOR PRINTED MATTER'S FUND RAISING EDITION.

December 2012.

I propose to bruise all the apples in all the shops in New York.

Peter Liversidge.

PROPOSAL FOR PRINTED MATTER INC.
195 10th AVENUE, NEW YORK, NY 10011, U.S.A.
FOR PRINTED MATTER'S FUND RAISING EDITION.
December 2012.

I propose to invite the musicians Rachel Grimes and Christopher Tignor to collaborate on five pieces of music for Printed Matter's store at 195 10th Avenue. The pieces can be of any length they will be played in the store at 5pm every day, one a day, Monday to Friday. They will be played for the first week of every month from January to December.

Peter Liversidge.

PROPOSAL FOR PRINTED MATTER INC.

195 10th AVENUE, NEW YORK, NY 10011, U.S.A.

FOR PRINTED MATTERS FUND RAISING EDITION.

December 2012.

I propose to post an edition of 5 mops to Printed Matter at the above address. The mops will be bought from a cleaner's shop here in London and posted without packaging to Printed Matter.

Peter Liversidge.

PROPOSAL FOR PRINTED MATTER INC.

195 10th AVENUE, NEW YORK, NY 10011, U.S.A.

FOR PRINTED MATTER'S FUNDRAISING EDITION.

December 2012.

I propose to employ a tattoo artist to operate from the Printed Matter store on 10th Avenue. I would ask the tattooist to work the same hours as the shop staff. The tattooist would be asked to realise an edition of 100 tattoos, the tattoos would be of a wrinkle.

Peter Liversidge.

PROPOSAL FOR PRINTED MATTER INC.
195 10th AVENUE, NEW YORK, 10011, U.S.A.
FOR THE PRINTED MATTER FUND RAISING EDITION.
December 2012.

I propose that this proposal should be reproduced as a poster to promote the Printed Matter Fund Raising Edition. The poster will be A0 size (1189 x 841mm / 46.8 x 33.1 inches) produced in an edit -ion of 500. 400 posters will be fly posted around American cities from New York to Boston, Miami to Minneapolis, Los Angeles to Seatt -le. The remaining posters will be sold through the Printed Matter shop at 195 10th Avenue, New York.

Peter Liversidge.

PROPOSAL FOR PRINTED MATTER INC.

195 10th AVENUE, NEW YORK, NY 10011, U.S.A.

FOR PRINTED MATTER'S FUND RAISING EDITION.

December 2012.

I propose to produce a small publication for the non-profit organization dedicated to the promotion of publications made by artists; Printed Matter. The publication will consist of a single colour polaroid of the exterior of the shop, taken from the curb on 10th Avenue. The interior of the shop/reading room would be documented on the same day using only black and white polaroid film.
The resulting photographs would be collated together in a small publication accompanied by a short story written by an invited writer.

Peter Liversidge.

PROPOSAL FOR PRINTED MATTER INC.

195 10th AVENUE, NEW YORK, NY 10011, U.S.A.

FOR THE PRINTED MATTER FUNDRAISING EDITION.

December 2012.

I propose to re-type this proposal 25 times. Each of the 25 copies will be typed as a copy of what you are now reading; with every typ--o, crossing out and error replicated 25 times. The resulting 25 copies will be given to a gilder who I will invite to guild this proposal from top to bottom using silver leaf. The entire surface area of this proposal will be obscured.

Peter Liversidge.

PROPOSAL FOR PRINTED MATTER INC.
195 10th AVENUE, NEW YORK, NY 10011, U.S.A.
FOR PRINTED MATTER'S FUND RAISING EDITION.
December 2012.

I propose to make a neon text piece for Printed Matter's Fund raising edition. The text piece will be an edition of all the states in America produced as a simple 5mm gauge neon text. Each state will only be fabricated once starting with Alabama, then Alaska; and so on, until all the states, ordered in alphabetical order, have been made once; ending with the final pair; Wisconsin, and finally Wyoming.
The 5mm gauge neon will be fabricated using white neon.

Peter Liversidge.

PROPOSAL FOR PRINTED MATTER INC.
195 10th AVENUE, NEW YORK, NY 10011, U.S.A.
FOR PRINTED MATTER'S FUND RAISING EDITION.
December **2012**.

I propose to produce an edition of a commercially produced roadsign. The sign used is one normally as a 'split sign' for parking, instruc-tions, and general close direction. The top of the sign is block colour with the text in white and the bottom of the sign is white, in a 50/50 split, The text in the white area of the sign always takes it's colour from the 'block' colour in the top 50% of the sign.
The sign will read: Will History Be Kind.
In the top (black) 50% the text will read: Will History.
In the bottom (white) 50% the text will read: Be Kind.

Peter Liversidge.

PROPOSAL FOR PRINTED MATTER INC.

195 10th AVENUE, NEW YORK, NY 10011, U.S.A.

FOR A PRINTED MATTER FUND RAISING EDITION.

December 2012.

I propose to produce an edition of contact lenses, the contact len -ses will match my eyes exactly. The lenses will match not only the colour but my focal length of each eye.

Peter Liversidge.

PROPOSAL FOR PRINTED MATTER INC.

195 10th AVENUE, NEW YORK, NY 10011, U.S.A.

FOR THE PRINTED MATTER FUND RAISING EDITION.

December 2012.

I propose to build doppelganger Printed Matter shops in other cities across the United States. Each of the doppelganger shops/stores would have exactly the same footprint as the Printed Matter store at 195 10th Avenue in New York. Each host city can apply for one of an edition of 5 doppelganger stores/shops, which will all have doppelganger stock based on what is to be found at 195 10th Avenue.

Peter Liversidge.

PROPOSAL FOR PRINTED MATTER INC.

195 10th AVENUE, NEW YORK, NY 10011, U.S.A.

FOR A PRINTED MATTER FUNDRAISING EDITION.

December 2012.

I propose to produce a bumper sticker for Printed Matter. The bump-er sticker would be produced in an edition of 1000.
250 of the 1000 stickers would be taken out into New York at night, and under the cover of darkness they will be attatched to the bump-ers of any city of New York municipal vehicle; from road sweepers to rubbish trucks, buses to bikes.
The bumper sticker would read: Everything is Connected.

Peter Liversidge.

PROPOSAL FOR PRINTED MATTER INC.

195 10th AVENUE, NEW YORK, NY 10011, U.S.A.

FOR PRINTED MATTER'S FINDRAISING EDITION.

December 2012.

I propose to produce a canvas bag in an edition of 100 for the Printed Matter fundraising edition. The bag will have a reproduc- -tion of this proposal on one side and on the other I will invent a logo/emblem for printed matter which will include the following text: Printed Matter - reincorporated 1978.

Peter Liversidge.

PROPOSAL FOR PRINTED MATTER INC.
195 10th AVENUE, NEW YORK, NY 10011, U.S.A.
FOR PRINTED MATTER'S FUNDRAISING EDITION.
December 2012.

I propose to ask the staff at printed matter to draw up a daily rota which includes all members of staff. The rota will be stri-ctly observed for exactly twelve months from it's starting point. The staff should organise the rota by simple classification of age eldest to youngest. The task would be to drop a single quarter every day on the pavement/side walk outside the shop on 10th Ave-nue. This should be done everyday the shop is open.

Peter Liversidge.

PROPOSAL FOR PRINTED MATTER INC.

195 10th AVENUE, NEW YORK, NY 10011, U.S.A.

FOR PRINTED MATTER'S FUNDRAISING EDITION.

December 2012.

I propose to collate all the proposals sent to Printed Matter Inc. in a book work.

Peter Liversidge.

PROPOSAL FOR PRINTED MATTER INC.
195 10th AVENUE, NEW YORK, NY 10011, U.S.A.
FOR THE PRINTED MATTER FUNDRAISING EDITION.
December 2012.

I propose to cast the small piece of flint I've been carrying aro--und in my front pocket for the past 14 months. I will cast the flint in solid silver, uncoated so that they can be hand polished by each owner and tarnish in their new location.

Peter Liversidge.

PROPOSAL FOR PRINTED MATTER INC.
195 10th AVENUE, NEW YORK, NY 10011, U.S.A.
FOR A PRINTED MATTER FUNDRAISING EDITION.
December 2012.

I propose that on 15th March 2015, I will take responsibility for the entire contents of the New York Times. The work will consist of all the articles, advertising, text, photographs, cartoons and weather reports enclosed in that Sunday's edition will now assume to be my/the work. The newspaper will be supported by an edition of 50 facsimile copies of this proposal, which will act as certificate to the work. The edit--ion of 50 will only be validated as part of the edition when accompa--nied by a copy of this proposal.

Peter Liversidge.

PROPOSAL FOR PRINTED MATTER INC.

195 10th AVENUE, NEW YORK, NY 10011, U.S.A.

FOR PRINTED MATTER'S FUNDRAISING EDITION.

December 2012.

I propose to bootleg my entire record collection on CD-R and offer it for sale through Printed Matter.

Peter Liversidge.

PROPOSAL FOR PRINTED MATTER INC.
195 10th AVENUE, NEW YORK, NY 10011, U.S.A.
FOR PRINTED MATTER'S FUND RAISING EDITION.
December 2012.

I propose to invite visitors to Printed Matter at the above address to take part in a performance piece. The piece in question is a re-working of the work: 'Gin Performance'
Gin Performance, when realised, consists of the following:

Gin, Tonic, Ice & Cucumber.
Gin Stand & White Bunting,
Staff & Uniforms, Editioned Glasses
(etched with the date, edition No.
and the word 'GIN')

The performance lasts for the duration of the gin, once it runs out the performance is over. The gin used should be the gin voted the best gin in the world; by The Wall Street Journal in 2003, that gin was: Hendricks Gin.

Peter Liversidge.

PROPOSAL FOR PRINTED MATTER INC.

195 10th AVENUE, NEW YORK, NY 10011, U.S.A.

FOR PRINTED MATTER'S FUNDRAISING EDITION.

December 2012.

I propose to edition an animated text piece. The text piece will be the alliteration: ping-pong.

The text is chosen not for it's reference to table tennis, but for the sound it makes in the mind and lips of each reader. The text: ping-pong will be reproduced in 8mm gauge H-37 Pink neon tubing. It will be animated so that it follows the sequence:

ping	-	on
ping	-	off
-pong	-	on
-pong	-	off
ping-pong	-	on
ping-pong	-	off

The sequence will start again.

Peter Liversidge.

PROPOSAL FOR PRINTED MATTER INC.

195 10th AVENUE, NEW YORK, NY 10011, U.S.A.

FOR PRINTED MATTER'S FUNDRAISING EDITION.

December 2012.

I propose to produce a print as a fundraising edition for Printed Matter.

Peter Liversidge.

PROPOSAL FOR PRINTED MATTER INC.
195 10th AVENUE, NEW YORK, NY 10011, U.S.A.
FOR PRINTED MATTER'S FUNDRAISING EDITION.
December 2012.

I propose that in the summer we will all get together for a picnic in central park.

Peter Liversidge.

PROPOSAL FOR PRINTED MATTER INC.

195 10th AVENUE, NEW YORK, NY, 10011, U.S.A.

FOR THE PRINTED MATTER FUNDRAISING EDITION.

December 2012.

I propose to collect a small branch from a European Beech tree grow--ing in Central Park. The branch would be cast in black bronze, so that it would be able to be inserted in a hole in the wall, as if it were growing out of that hole.

Peter Liversidge.

PROPOSAL FOR PRINTED MATTER INC.
195 10th AVENUE, NEW YORK, NY 10011, U.S.A.
FOR PRINTED MATTER'S FUNDRAISING EDITION.
December 2012.

I propose that we take a walk together.

Peter Liversidge.

PROPOSAL FOR PRINTED MATTER INC.
195 10th AVENUE, NEW YORK, 10011, U.S.A.
FOR PRINTED MATTER'S FUNDRAISING EDITION.
December 2012.

I propose that the wind will bend.

Peter Liversidge.

PROPOSAL FOR PRINTED MATTER INC.

195 10th AVENUE, NEW YORK, NY 10011, U.S.A.

FOR THE PRINTED MATTER FUNDRAISING EDITION.

December 2012.

I propose to make casts of the cracks in the shop floor at Printed Matter at 195 10th Avenue. The resulting casts would be used to produce aluminium copies of the cracks and holes in the floor. The resulting interconnecting aluminium structures will be wall mounted within Printed Matter at the above address.

Peter Liversidge.

PROPOSAL FOR PRINTED MATTER INC.
195 10th AVENUE, NEW YORK, NY 10011, U.S.A.
FOR PRINTED MATTER'S FUNDRAISING EDITION.
December 2012.

I propose to realise an edition of falling. The edition will be realised at the point at which it is bought from Printed Matter as part of it's fundraising edition. I will give Printed Matter a mobile phone number which after the point of sale they will text me to let me know that I should fall. Once on the ground I will photograph whatever is infront of me. Whatever it is that is photographed becomes part of the edition and that image is authen--ticated by a copy of this proposal.

Peter Liversidge.

DATES

01 December 2012

02 December 2012.

Published by Printed Matter, Inc., 2014
In an edition of 500 copies

Peter Liversidge would like to thank:
Cassie Liversidge, George & Thomas Liversidge, Gary Arber,
The Brothers, Levin Haegele, Sophie Pasiewicz, Keith Gray, James
Jenkin and all at Printed Matter, Inc., Christopher Tignor, Katya Pronin, Darbyshire
Framemakers, Conveyor Arts, Richard & Florence Ingleby and all at Ingleby Gallery,
Sean Kelly, Lauren Kelly and all at Sean Kelly Gallery.

Printed and bound by Conveyor Arts

ISBN: 978-0-89439-075-3

peterliversidge.com

Printed Matter, Inc.
195 Tenth Ave
New York, NY 10011
www.printedmatter.org

Printed Matter, Inc. is an independent 501(c)3 non-profit organization founded in 1976 by artists and art workers with the mission to foster the appreciation, dissemination, and understanding of artists' books and other artists' publications.

Printed Matter, Inc.

NOTES

NOTES

NOTES

NOTES